The Meanie Genie

**Daddy's stories are the best,
They're always going to
beat the rest!**

I do love when it's time for bed, for when it's time to rest my head.

My daddy comes up to read a book, I sit up straight, to have a better look.

Sometimes when he reads, said Billy, Daddy makes the story silly.

Other times he reads the story, Daddy makes the story gory.

But here he comes, I cannot wait, to see which story is my fate.

Tonight said Dad the story I tell,
Is one that is known to all, very well...

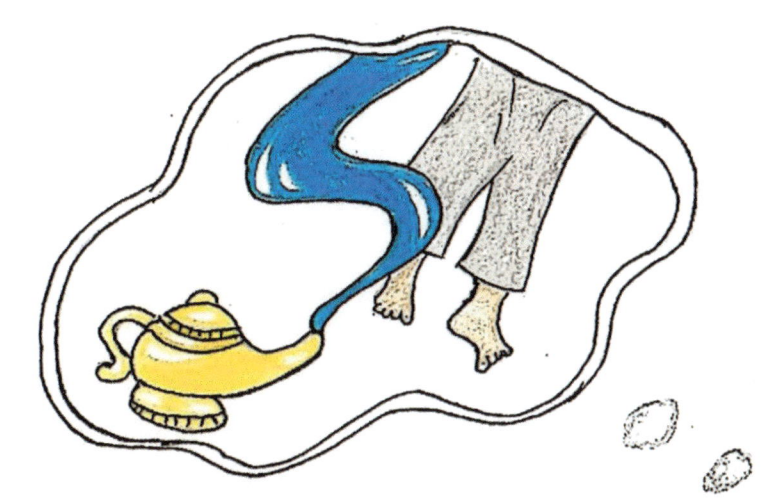

Well, a version you heard, but that was a lie, Of the Genie, a magical lamp, and a guy.

Well, the story begins with a young group of Four, Who all said that they wanted more!

They found a map of treasures and a cave, And they all decided they were feeling brave.

They set off now on a hunt for the treasure, But the trouble they would find would be hard to measure.

The four friends left on the journey together, Lucky for them it was quite nice weather.

They came to a cave that they found on the map,
And they said to each other "Careful, there could be a trap."

They ventured inside the deep dark cave,
And the group of four felt a bit less brave.

But they ventured on with eyes on the prize, they turned a corner and got a surprise.

For in the roof, a hole big and round, the light from the moon shone onto the ground.

When the moon was high and shining bright, and the stars were gleaming in the night,

They saw a strange and wonderful sight, it was a golden egg that shone so bright,

With a strange and eery glimmering light.

As they crept close to have a look,

Luke caught his foot on a hidden nook.

Whilst stumbling forward towards the ground,

He knocked the egg that they had found.

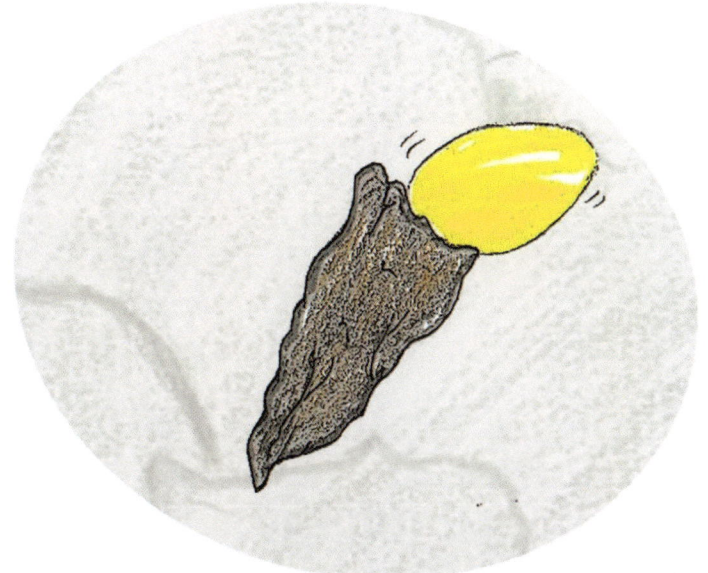

**It rolled around and hit his feet,
Then bellowed out a terrible heat.**

**A deafening crack and a cloud of smoke,
And all around began to splutter and choke.**

A booming voice came through the cloud,
The voice was deep and incredibly loud!

"I grant 1 wish each, to the ones with the egg,
But think very carefully please I beg,

For the wishes I grant cannot be undone,
And people before you made wishes quite dumb!"

As the smoke cleared, they saw in the room,
A giant floating man who spoke with a boom.

He looked at them coldly and said with a grin,
"So, which of you wants to make a wish, let's begin!"

Jack stepped forward looking quite small,

Looked at the Genie and said, "Make me 10 feet tall".

Genie looked down and said, "As you wish,"

He gestured toward him and gave a big swish.

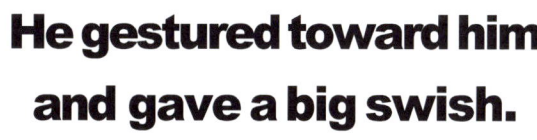

Smoke blew around him, the group looked around,

**For where their friend stood,
10 feet stood on the ground!**

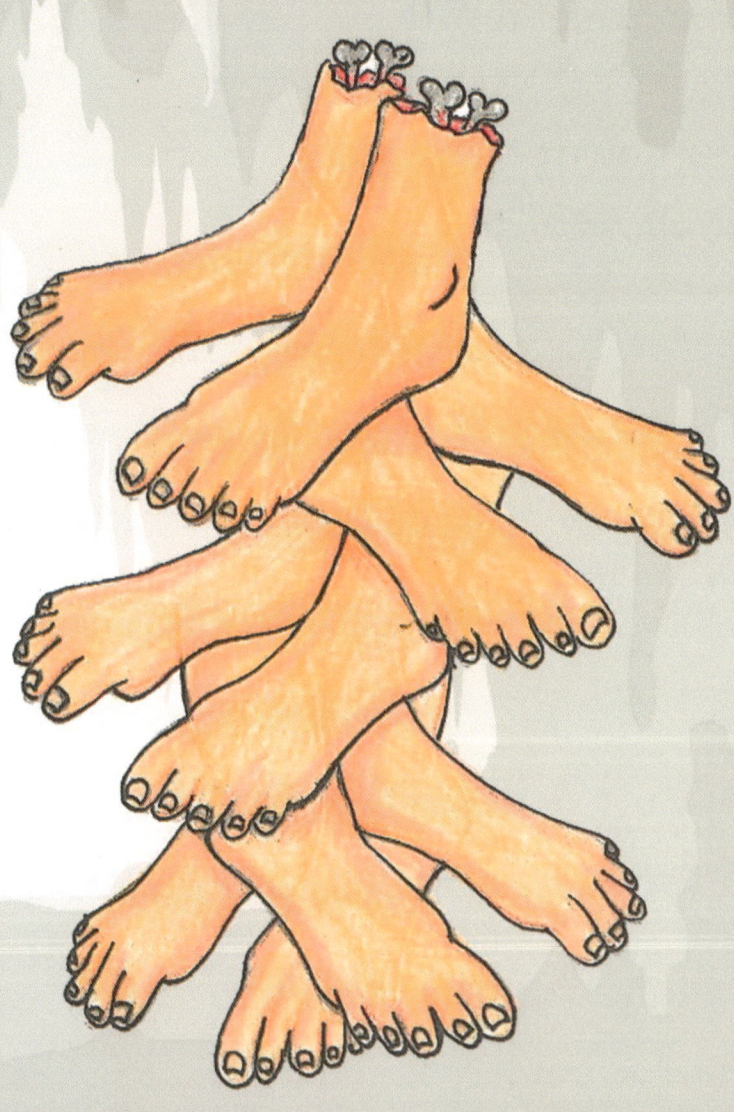

"What have you done?"
the group screamed at the Genie,
"What have you done to our friend, you Meaney?"

The giant man turned
and looked at the group, and said,
"Careful now or I'll turn you to soup,

Now warnings I gave you,
now I recommend,
before you wish,
consult with your friend!"

Brook stepped forward saying "Don't be absurd".
"None of us trust that you'll keep your word!"

Now I wish to fly, and don't mess around,
I want to be able to float off the ground,

And fly all about, and not even think,
About how my feet are beginning to stink."

Genie looked down and said, "As you wish,"

He gestured toward her and gave a big swish.

Again, came the smoke, this wasn't new,

But stood where their friend was, was a fly around poo!

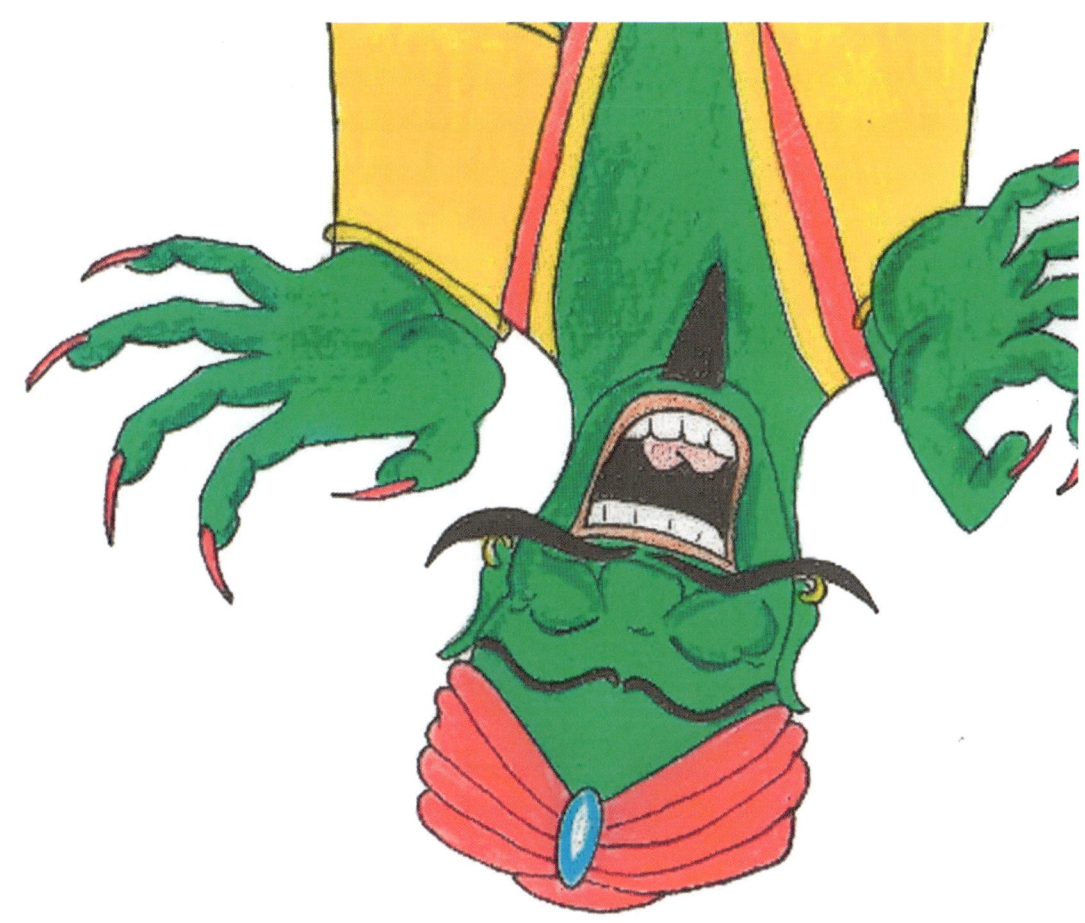

The Genie looked down and started to chuckle,
Then said to the group "You are starting to buckle!"

"Twice I have warned not to rush what you say,"
"Looks like nobody's leaving today!"

The 2 friends remaining looked at each other,
Then realized that they must wish for another.

Now Luke stepped forward and said full of grace,

"I really do miss seeing their face,"

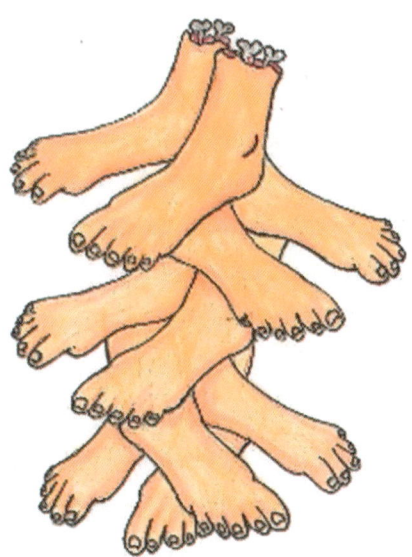

"Please bring them back genie, now I do beg,"

"Even though one is now barely a leg."

Genie looked down and said, "As you wish,"

He gestured toward him and gave a big swish.

Now, the same thing happened, as before,
But when the smoke cleared, they saw nothing more,

He turned to the genie and said, "What the heck?"
"You're starting to be, a pain in my neck!"

"I made a wish for my friends to be back,"
"And your magic is lame, you don't have the knack."

Then 2 voices he heard from behind him he found,
That made him turn round to the familiar sound.

"It's the others I hear them, I can hear Jack!"
Then Billy screams "Look! It's moving on your back!"

He lifted his shirt, Billy started to shout,

The friends we have lost, they are starting to sprout!"

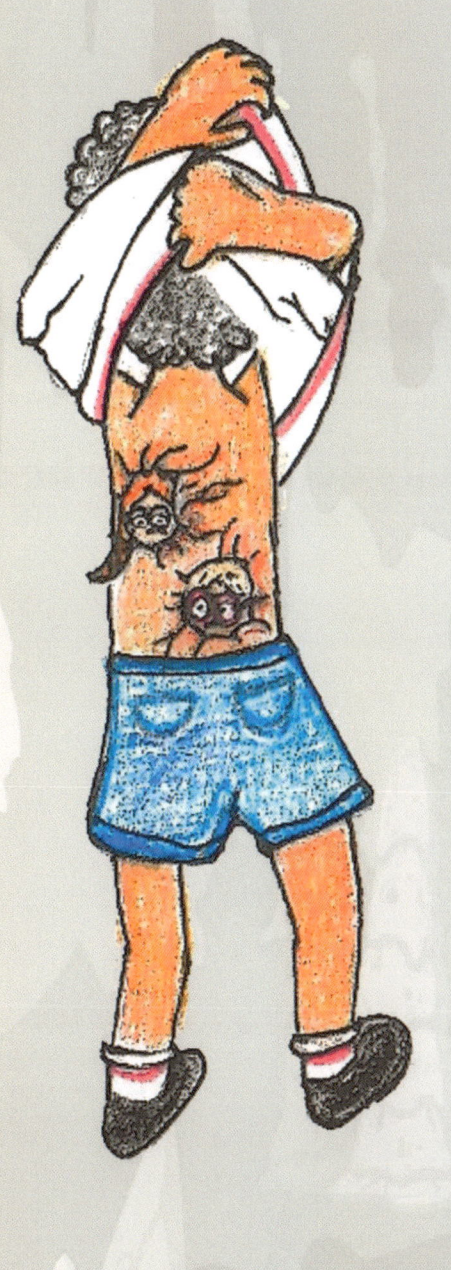

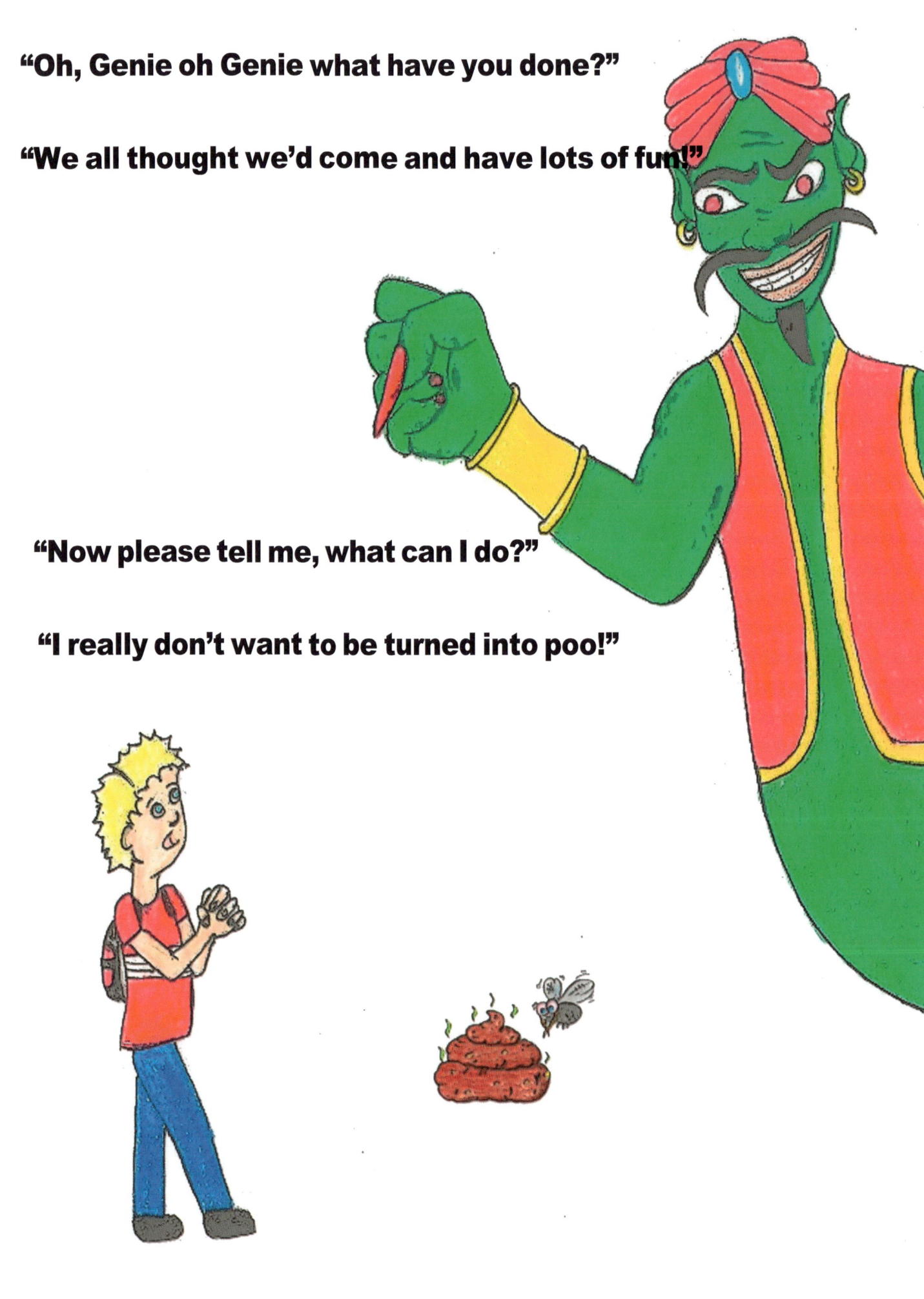

"One wish you have left, now say and be done!" "I'm bored now, it's fun, but like the others you're all dumb!"

Billy stepped forward and said with a smile, "Now Genie I think that you've been here a while."

"The wish that I want to be mine I must say," "Is I wish that we'd chose not to come here today!"

"To be home snuggled up, all warm in my bed, "Getting ready to rest my sleepy head,"

"Waiting for Daddy to read a book," "And I can sit up to have a look!"

Genie looked down and said, "As you wish,"

He gestured toward him and gave a big swish.

**Mummy and Daddy look down and smiled,
As they looked at their beautiful sleeping child,**

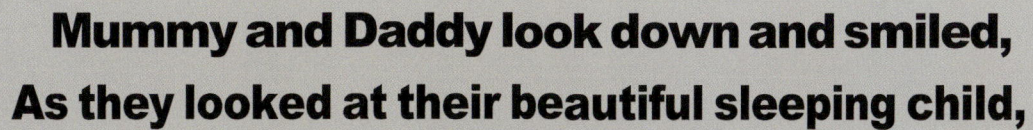

**They gave him a kiss, whispered sweet dreams and goodnight,
Then blew one more kiss, as they turned out the lig**

This book is dedicated to my amazing wife and children, who support me through everything and make every day brilliant.

Also a special thank you to L.B. who has been a huge help throughout.

I've always loved reading stories to my children at bedtime, and regularly changed the stories to make them a little cheekier.

I hope you enjoyed my story. There are plenty more to come.

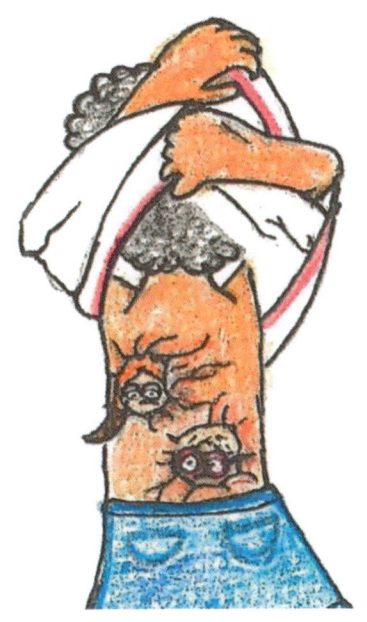

Printed in Great Britain
by Amazon